D1067985

BEAVER STREAM

SMITHSONIAN
WILD HERITAGE COLLECTION

EASY
H

For my grandchildren
— M. H.

To Ann and Woody,
thanks for your help and love,
with forever love
— D. K.

Copyright © 1994 by Trudy Management Corporation,
165 Water Street, Norwalk, CT 06856 and the Smithsonian Institution,
Washington, DC 20560.

Soundprints is a Division of Trudy Management Corporation, Norwalk, Connecticut.

All rights reserved. No part of this book may be reproduced or
transmitted in any form or by any means whatsoever without prior
written permission of the publisher.

Book Design: Shields & Partners, Westport, CT

First Edition
10 9 8 7 6 5 4 3 2 1
Printed in Singapore

Acknowledgements:
    Our very special thanks to Dr. Charles Handley of the department of
vertebrate zoology at the Smithsonian's National Museum of Natural History
for his curatorial review.

Library of Congress Cataloging-in-Publication Data

Holmer, Marilyn F.

Beaver stream / by Marilyn F. Holmer ;
illustrated by David Kiehm.
        p.   cm.
Summary: During the winter, Beaver searches for a home, flees a coyote,
and finds a mate.
        ISBN 1-56899-059-6
1. Beavers — Juvenile fiction. [1. Beavers — Fiction. 2. Winter — Fiction.]
I. Kiehm, David, ill. II. Title.
        PZ10.3.H7275Be 1994   94-1768
        (E) — dc20   CIP
                                                               AC

ST. MARYS PUBLIC LIBRARY

BEAVER STREAM

by Marilyn F. Holmer
Illustrated by David Kiehm

Soundprints
Where Children Discover Nature

A cold night wind rustles the cattails at
Blackwater Marsh. The snowshoe hare shivers
in her willow nook. A muskrat family snuggles
together in their house of reeds. And frogs bury
themselves in the soft mud of the stream bed.

Beaver swims in the icy water. He is
alone, separated from his family in a raging
flood. Having lost his lodge also, he must now find a
new home before the harsher winter weather settles in.
Silently, Beaver slips into a dive. Beads of silver
bubbles flow from his fur.

Swimming to the surface to check for danger, Beaver sniffs the air. He is not alone anymore. In the moonlight, he sees another beaver family busily preparing for winter. They plaster their lodge with mud to keep out chilling winds. Nearby, they stock a pile of branches and shrubs on the pond bottom. This will be their food supply when marsh ice seals the beavers in their underwater home during the long cold winter.

Suddenly Beaver hears a tail slap. "Thwack!"
An older beaver warns him to stay away! Beaver is not
welcome. He turns and swims quickly up the stream.

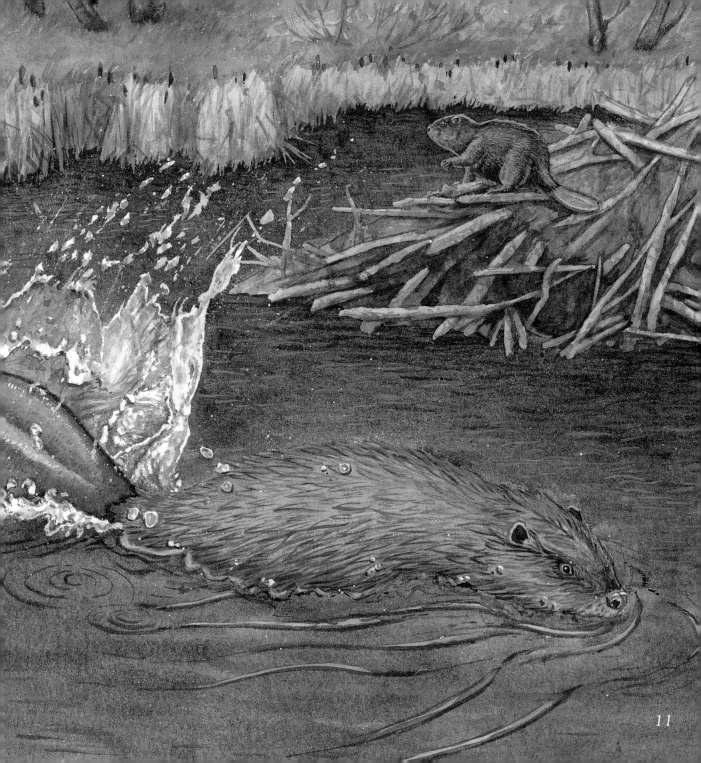

Around a bend, behind a stand of cattails, the stream widens into a woodland pond. Aspen, Beaver's favorite food tree, grows along its banks. He circles the pond, listening. A lone coyote howls from the surrounding hills. Beaver waits. But only the wind sweeps through the trees.

Ice already clings to the reed-grasses. There is much work to do, and not enough time to build a snug lodge like the one he was raised in.

He dives to the bottom of the pond and glides over to the bank. Beneath the roots of the trees, Beaver begins to dig an entrance to his bank burrow. Upward and upward to dry earth he will tunnel. At the tunnel's end he will construct a sleeping room with a small air vent.

Beaver completes his new burrow in a few nights. Very, very hungry, he floats to the surface of the pond and sniffs the wind for signs of danger. Sensing it is safe, he clambers up the bank toward the aspen trees.

He clips off a tender branch with his sharp teeth and eats the bark. Then he cuts another branch. Clenching it in his teeth, he dives to the pond bottom near the entrance to his burrow. He buries it in the mud, beginning his own stockpile of branches for winter food.

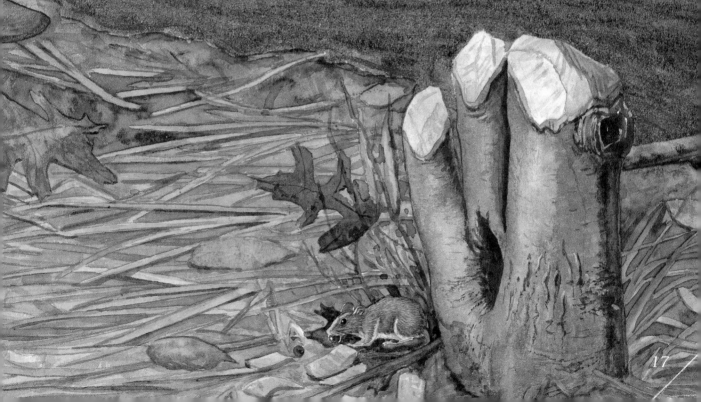

Beaver returns to the woods to gather more branches. Often, he stops gnawing to listen and test the air. He hears a whisper of a sound. Is that the wind rustling the grasses? Close by, in the shadows, a hungry coyote crouches behind a log and waits. Beaver sniffs the rising wind.

Suddenly, the coyote leaps. Too late! Seeing his enemy, Beaver dodges out of the way. He charges through the grasses to the water's edge and jumps in. Snapping at his heels, the coyote dashes in after him.

21

Beaver slaps the water hard with his flat tail and dives. "KER-PLUNGE!" As the slap sprays water into the air, the startled coyote swims back to shore.

Stroking hard with his webbed hind feet, Beaver streaks underwater for a very long time. Racing from the danger, he leaves the coyote and his bank burrow far behind.

Finally, Beaver surfaces. He is in another strange place. A different wind funnels through the trees and ripples the grasses. Lying still in the water, he sniffs the air. A scent he knows well, beaver sweet, leads him to a beaver dam.

He listens. He tests the odors of the pond. Then Beaver sees her...a dark shape resting in the shadows of the small lodge. Cautiously, he approaches.

As Beaver paddles closer, the stranger watches. Then she dives into the water and swims ever so slowly towards him.

The moon sinks behind the trees. Its last slivers of light shine through the branches. Beaver and his new friend chatter happily as they playfully splash their tails.

Beaver follows his friend to her lodge. Tomorrow
they will begin to cut and store aspen branches
for their food pile. But now, they snuggle up
together inside their warm winter home
and go to sleep.

About the Beaver

The beaver is a distant cousin of the prehistoric giant beaver (<u>Castoroides</u>) that lived during the ice ages and weighed about 400 pounds. Today's beaver is a peaceful, semi-aquatic mammal and vegetarian that weighs about 55 pounds with a life span up to 20 years. Beavers can swim up to three miles per hour, and can remain under water for 15 minutes.

Mating for life, Beavers have three or four young called kits, born with their eyes open and fully furred. The first two years the young beavers stay with their parents. They learn to cut down trees to eat the young bark and build dams, lodges and winter food piles. Then they are ready to go off to start homes of their own.

Beavers are nature's hydraulic engineers. Their dams store water in ponds that benefit many other animals as well as man. Probably no other animal is more important for creating, protecting and preserving our wetlands than the beaver.

Glossary

air vent: An open space on the top of a beaver lodge or bank burrow where fresh air is circulated.

aspen: A hardwood tree that grows in sunny areas in cooler parts of North America. The aspen's range begins in Canada and extends as far south as Virginia and the mountains in Mexico.

bank burrow: A beaver home dug into the bank of a pond or stream.

cattails: Plants with long narrow leaves and brown furry spikes that grow in marshy places.

coyote: A wolf-like canid and member of the dog family found throughout much of North America.

lodge: A dome-shaped beaver house built in water and made from sticks and mud. It has a dry living area and an underwater entrance.

tunnel: A passageway through the ground.

webbed: Having skin between the toes for extra swimming power.

Points of Interest in this Book

pp. 4-5 snowshoe hare.

pp. 6-7, 14-15 brook trout.

pp. 8-9, 12-13 white-tailed deer.

pp. 12-13 mink; Beavers can smell aspen trees over 200 yards away.

pp. 14-15, 24-25 common shiners.

pp. 14-15 Beavers are adapted to working under water with special valves to keep water out of their noses and ears, clear eyelids to protect their eyes, and lips that close behind their front teeth so they can gnaw through roots underwater.

pp. 16-17, 18-19, 20-21 deer mouse.

pp. 26-27 great horned owl; "Beaver sweet" odors are scent mounds made of mud, leaves and beaver oils, made to mark their territories.

pp. 28-29 long-tailed weasel.

StM